Ela Area Public Library District
275 Mo

P9-CQV-783
www.

31241008843537

WITHDRAWN

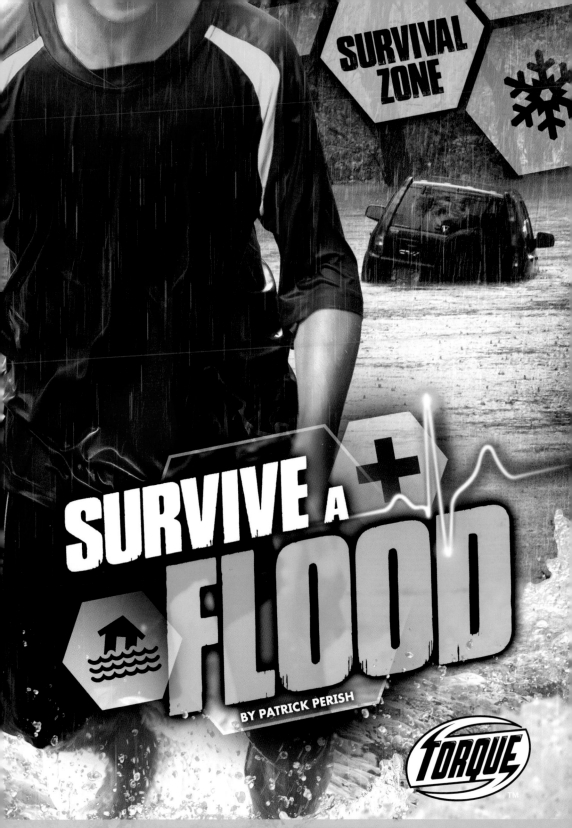

SURVIVAL ZONE

SURVIVE A FLOOD

BY PATRICK PERISH

TORQUE

BELLWETHER MEDIA · MINNEAPOLIS, MN

TM

Are you ready to take it to the extreme? Torque books thrust you into the action-packed world of sports, vehicles, mystery, and adventure. These books may include dirt, smoke, fire, and chilling tales. **WARNING** : read at your own risk.

This edition first published in 2017 by Bellwether Media, Inc.

No part of this publication may be reproduced in whole or in part without written permission of the publisher. For information regarding permission, write to Bellwether Media, Inc., Attention: Permissions Department, 5357 Penn Avenue South, Minneapolis, MN 55419.

Library of Congress Cataloging-in-Publication Data

Names: Perish, Patrick, author.
Title: Survive a Flood / by Patrick Perish.
Description: Minneapolis, MN : Bellwether Media, Inc., 2017. | Series:
   Torque: Survival Zone | Audience: Grades 3 through 7. | Includes
   bibliographical references and index.
Identifiers: LCCN 2015049938 | ISBN 9781626174429 (hardcover : alk.
paper)
Subjects: LCSH: Floods–Juvenile literature. | Floods–Safety
   measures–Juvenile literature. | Preparedness–Juvenile literature.
Classification: LCC HV609 .P447 2017 | DDC 613.6/9–dc23
LC record available at http://lccn.loc.gov/2015049938

Text copyright © 2017 by Bellwether Media, Inc. TORQUE and associated logos are trademarks and/or registered trademarks of Bellwether Media, Inc.

SCHOLASTIC, CHILDREN'S PRESS, and associated logos are trademarks and/or registered trademarks of Scholastic Inc.

Printed in the United States of America, North Mankato, MN.

TABLE OF CONTENTS

FLASH FLOOD!

On October 4, 2015, Mary Baylor was having trouble sleeping. It had rained heavily all night. She got up and looked out her window. A small creek ran through her backyard in Columbia, South Carolina. Normally shallow, the creek had swelled with rainwater. It rose over the banks and rushed toward the house. Mary hurried to wake her husband and children.

"We saw trees swept down like they were mere toothpicks."
-Mary Baylor

The Baylors headed out the door with overnight packs they had prepared earlier. Water was already flowing into the front yard. They made their way uphill to a friend's house.

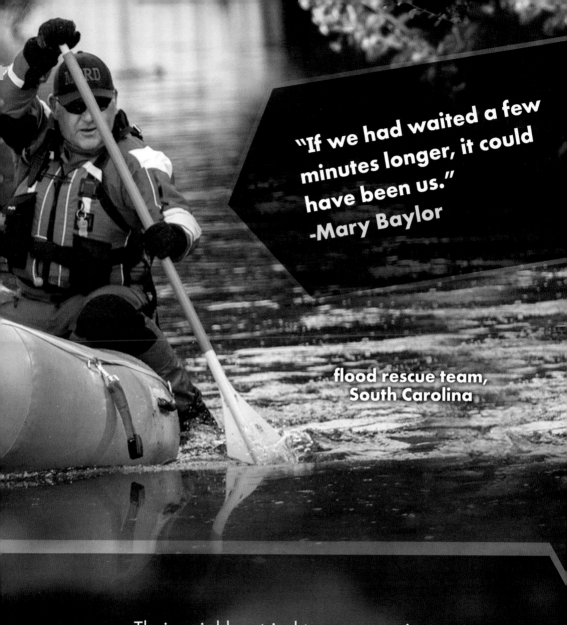

"If we had waited a few minutes longer, it could have been us."
-Mary Baylor

flood rescue team, South Carolina

Their neighbor tried to escape minutes later, but the water was too high. Emergency teams rescued him. South Carolina's record-breaking rains claimed 19 lives. Thanks to preparation and luck,

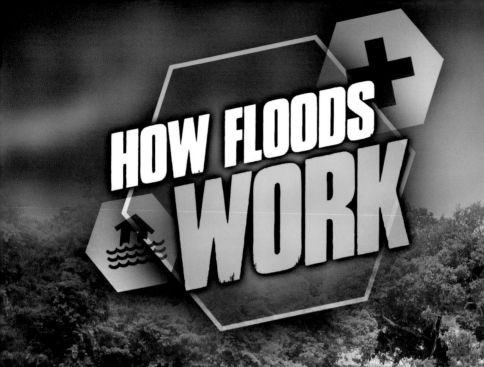

HOW FLOODS WORK

Flooding happens when an area receives more water than it can **absorb** at the time. This can be caused by heavy rainfall, rapid snowmelt, or events such as a dam breaking.

Usually there is some warning of flooding, but not always. A **flash flood** rises rapidly. Its powerful force can become deadly in minutes.

JOHNSTOWN FLOOD

In 1889, a dam near Johnstown, Pennsylvania burst. It sent a 40-foot (12-meter) wall of water slamming into the town.

Flooding can happen in places you would not expect. Dry desert **canyons** and mountain streams can rapidly overflow with water. Even on a cloudless day, rain far away might cause flooding near you.

Before hiking, check weather reports. Avoid narrow canyons if there is a risk of flooding.

HOW FLASH FLOODS HAPPEN

1. Heavy rain falls onto soaked ground

2. Ground cannot absorb rainfall so it runs into a river

3. River rises past its banks, causing a flood

RARE BLOOMS

Floods can be life-giving as well as deadly. Every five to seven years, flooding in the Atacama Desert causes it to burst into bloom.

BEFORE THE STORM

Every second counts during a flood. In a few minutes, water can overflow riverbanks. Making a plan beforehand will help you move fast.

Know the flood risk in your area and put together an emergency kit. Your family should choose a safe meeting place on high ground. Pick an emergency contact outside the area for everyone to call.

EMERGENCY KIT LIST

 dry or canned food

 bottled water

 emergency radio

 flashlight

 extra batteries

 first aid kit

 clothing

 matches

 candles

 blankets

 cash

 cell phone and charger

 road maps

 medications

EVACUATE!

When a flood is possible, listen for orders to **evacuate**. Severe storms may cause a **power outage**. Stay tuned to weather reports with a battery-powered radio.

CRANKED UP!

Low on batteries? Many emergency radios can be powered by a hand crank or sunlight.

As you evacuate, avoid walking through water, especially if it is moving. Just 6 inches (15 centimeters) of flowing water can knock you down. If you must, use a stick to check for solid ground beneath the water.

FLOOD WATCHES AND WARNINGS

FLOOD ADVISORY:
Minor flooding may occur and could cause problems.

FLOOD WATCH:
Conditions are right for a flood to occur. Keep updated on weather reports.

FLOOD WARNING:
A flood is happening or is about to happen. Follow instructions. Evacuate if necessary.

FLASH FLOOD WARNING:
A flash flood is about to happen. Get to higher ground immediately!

Drivers should never cross flooded roads. Rushing waters can pick up your car. It is also hard to tell what lies underwater. Roads may be damaged or **washed out**.

CRAZY CURRENTS

Moving water is very strong. It only takes 2 feet (0.6 meters) of it to carry away a car!

ESCAPING A CAR IN FLOODWATERS

STEP 1: Do not panic

STEP 2: Open windows or the door to escape

STEP 3: If neither opens, break a window with a sharp tool, removable headrest, or your foot

STEP 4: If window does not break, open the door when the water fills the car

STEP 5: Get to high ground!

If water surrounds your car, get out. Try to get to a higher **elevation**. If you are pulled into high water, point your feet downstream. Go over any obstacles, not under.

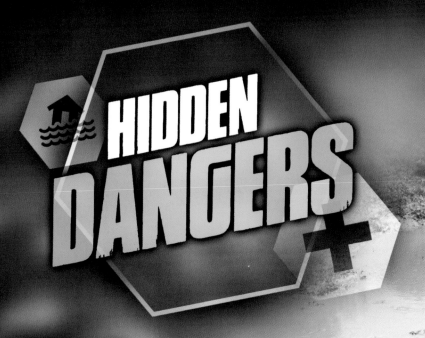

HIDDEN DANGERS

After the waters **recede**, dangers remain. Stay away from puddles and streams. **Debris** or downed power lines may hide under the water. Do not touch electrical equipment if it or you are wet. Doing so can cause a deadly shock.

Floodwaters are very dirty. They can contain **sewage** and harmful chemicals. Faucet water must be boiled until authorities give the all clear.

The Boston Post

22 Pages Today

THURSDAY, JANUARY 16, 1919

HUGE MOLASSES TAN
IN NORTH END; 11 D

Giant Wave of 2,300,000 Gallons of Molass
Everything Before It—100 Men, Women an
Sticky Stream—Buildings, Vehicles and L

35 STATES ON
DRY LAW LIST

Amendment Ratified by Five Yes-
terday—One More Needed—
Predict Nation Dry July 1

SECRECY
IN PEACE
CONGRESS

France, Italy and Japan
Outvote U. S. and
Britain

BOY'S STORY AID
TO MRS. LEDAUDV

A STICKY MESS

In 1919, Boston, Massachusetts, was hit with an unusual flood. A tank burst and spilled more than 2 million gallons (7.6 million liters) of molasses.

19

It can be dangerous to enter buildings after floods. They may **collapse** from the water damage. Keep out until they have been inspected.

Cleanup can take a long time. **Disinfect** anything that may have touched floodwaters. Some things, such as food, cannot be cleaned. These things can be replaced. Your most important job is to stay safe and survive the flood!

GLOSSARY

absorb—to take in or soak up

canyons—narrow valleys with steep sides

collapse—to fall apart

debris—the remains of something broken down or destroyed

disinfect—to cleanse of bacteria that might cause disease

elevation—height above sea level

evacuate—to leave a dangerous area

flash flood—an overflow of water that occurs within a few hours of heavy rainfall

power outage—a loss of electricity to an area

recede—to fall or pull back

sewage—human waste and waste water

washed out—swept away by water

AT THE LIBRARY

Dougherty, Terri. *The Worst Floods of All Time*. North Mankato, Minn.: Capstone Press, 2012.

Hamilton, S.L. *Floods*. Minneapolis, Minn.: ABDO Pub. Co., 2012.

Portman, Michael. *Deadly Floods*. New York, N.Y.: Gareth Stevens Pub., 2012.

ON THE WEB

Learning more about surviving a flood is as easy as 1, 2, 3.

1. Go to www.factsurfer.com.

2. Enter "survive a flood" into the search box.

3. Click the "Surf" button and you will see a list of related web sites.

With factsurfer.com, finding more information is just a click away.

INDEX

The images in this book are reproduced through the courtesy of: staticnak, front cover (person); Bonnie Watton, front cover (background); zlenzlla, pp. 4-5; Andor Bujdoso, p. 5 (window); faestock, p. 5 (woman); Jason Lee/ The Sun News/ AP Images, pp. 6-7; BABYFRUITY, pp. 8-9; Niday Picture Library/ Alamy, p. 9; jakubcejpek, p. 10; emattil, p. 10 (left); Oleg Pogozhikh, p. 10 (right); Kseniya Ragozina, p. 11; Stefan Siems, p. 12; Deposit Photos/ Glow Images, p. 13; Adrian Sherratt/ Alamy, pp. 14-15; josefkubes, pp. 16-17; Dave Wheeler, p. 17; Jack Schiffer, p. 18 (left); EdStock, p. 18 (right); Joanna Dorota, pp. 18-19; Boston Post/ Wikipedia, p. 19; Baloncici, p. 20; ZUMA Press/ Alamy, p. 21.